GOD WHISPERS TO ME

Poetry By Starr

JENISE HYLTON

TABLE OF CONTENTS

FOREWARD

My best friend for life, Jenise Lady Hylton, now known as Starr, for she is known in many sister circles. Me and Lady, (that is the name I know her by), met over 30 years ago. We met in 1983 in August Martin H.S. in Southside Queens. We spent time together cutting class so that we could play handball on the handball courts, which happened to be right outside of the principal's office window, but we played anyway. One day the principal invited our parents up to the school, and they all watched us cut class on the handball court. Eventually they kicked me out and I transferred to John Adams, and Lady transferred as well. Well, all I can say was our high school years got crazy. We stopped cutting class and just played hooky all together. We were caught up in that substance abuse era, but through it all, we made it through. We separated, went our own ways, and started doing our own thing. Years went by, but we would always reconnect, and we remained in constant contact with each other. Both of us graduated from college and from different junctions in our lives. We have graduated from being Ding Bats, (that is the name her mother gave to us in high school). Our friendship has lasted through the test of times. My dearest friend for life has evolved into a wonderful, deep persona that manifest her truest quality, Poetry. This talented writer of poetry has touched my consciousness for many years. Through her words she writes, and through her poetry she speaks she is so passionate. I have encouraged her for years to share it, get it out there so that the world can hear. The language she uses is clear and intelligible to the average person for consumption. I have always been a personal fan and beneficiary of the wisdom of her writings of inner peace and the understandings to life/s complexities. My friend Lady is a deep thinker.

She has true emotional connections to feelings of love, anger, life social norms, but mostly to Spirituality. It is my hope that the consumers of this book of poetry will gain personal insights that will inspire, fulfill, and promote self awareness. My dearest friend, I wish you every bit of success that is surely to come your way. Hoping your words will inspire others as they have me.

Love Always
Gwendolyn Landis

PREFACE

This book of poetry is about my feelings through my life's experiences. Growing up in life I was not outspoken. I really did not know how to express myself, so I kept a lot in as I went along with the crowd. At times I felt phony because I did not know how to face my true reality. At times I did not see me, I could see everyone else in me, but I could not see myself, that was because I was trying to be like everyone else, instead of just being myself. When I started writing my poetry, it was like I found myself. It felt strange how I was able to express myself more so to a piece of paper, being able to write down things that I could not sit and talk to anyone about. It was because I knew that the pieces of paper would not judge me. But seeing my feelings on paper made them more of a reality to me every time I read them. Poetry is an expression of feelings; some poetry differs from others. You have some that rhyme, some that do not, some that are true, and some that are not. My poetry in this book is about my true life's experiences. So now through my poetry and vocally, I am outspoken. Poetry is healing for me, because I can express myself, even if it is to a piece of paper. These are my true feelings from my heart. So, through my poetry and my feelings I can bleed out, cry out and purge out all of the discomfort, animosity, hate and jealousy that is in my heart and replace it with love. I named this book God Whispers To Me, because anytime I feel myself going through something or just having a bad day and I feel as if I just can not do it, God whispers to me Philippians 4:13 which is I can do all things through Christ who strengthens me. He always reminds me of where he has brought me from as well as where he is taking me. God has changed my heart and my life, and he continues to change it in a unique way.

The initials **LOH.LM.JH** at the end of each poem stands for
LOH Love **O**va **H**ate This is how my grandma felt about life. She Loved.
LM Little **M**ary I am my mothers child, you can see her in me
JH Jenise **H**ylton The author

Some of my poems will have an introduction before the actual poem, it will explain a little of what the poem is about. I hope you will enjoy me inside of my poetry.

LOH.LM.JH

INTRODUCTION

I am the Poetic writer Starr
And in my thoughts, I have so much to say
As I think about my life's experiences
And how I dealt with them each and every day
I take all of those experiences
And I put them into words
All of my feelings, my up, and my downs
On these pieces of paper my life I purge
Because as I write down my thoughts, I get intimate
When it comes to a piece of paper and a pen
As I take my pen and it rolls across the paper
Writing about my now's and my then
Because on these pieces of paper is where I put all of my tears
And on these pieces of paper is where I face all of my fears
On these pieces of paper for me it is always there
To console all of my notes even when no one else cares
These pieces of paper give me space
After each word
These pieces of paper remember every words I say
As it holds all of my concerns
These pieces of paper know all of my secrets
That no one else knows about me
These pieces of paper know my struggles with addictions
My hurts and all of my miseries
But these pieces of paper will also tell you
About the love God has given to me

These pieces of paper will tell you about
How he has blessed me and made me see
So as these pieces of paper lays there blank
And waits for me patiently
To fill the blanks in with a story
That is just all about me
So please enjoy my journey
Of my life and its different roles
Please enjoy reading from these pieces of paper
Where I have put down all of my soul

LOH.LM.JH

INTRODUCTION TO THE PATH I CHOSE FOR ME

This poem is about the path I chose growing up. My life in the beginning always seemed to be on a path toward destruction. I was always trying hard to be like other people, instead of making it easy by just being myself. I always cared about what people thought, and I tried to make everyone happy except for myself. That was hard, because trying to make everyone happy was sometimes good and sometimes bad. It was good because people are happy when you are pleasing them all of the time, and bad because those same people you are pleasing will end up using and abusing you. Then you are unhappy trying to make them happy. The most important thing I have learned through all of my paths was who I could trust, who will be there for me, and most of all who loved me. It was God and my family all of the time. I leaned more on God because he gave me no judgement in the things I did. But to see any disappointments in the faces of my family would have been hard. Through all of my paths God has given me wisdom. God sent me through things that only he could bring me out of. He wanted to show me that he is, and will forever be in control. Your path is how you make it, it could be an easy one or a hard one, that is your choice. But the main thing is through it all you learn from it. I chose the hard way growing up, but I still came out in a good way and that is Gods way.

LOH.LM.JH

THE PATH I CHOSE FOR ME

The streets were my path, I tried not to want
I slept in the gutter, and I lived like a runt
I ran with the thieves I fed my soul negativity
I walked through life distraughtly
All because of the path I chose for me....
I went toe to toe with evil
I went face to face with ungodly people
Men women black white
Some people not even legal
But my family, my crew, and my weapons
They took incredibly loving care of me
They were the only ones
Who was actually there for me
They placed a kiss on my head
To show their love for me
Through my sadness and all of my miseries
All because of the path I chose for me......
The path that I chose for me
It was not supposed to incriminate me
But those were the valleys
That my father had chosen for me
It was not supposed to have been negative

It was supposed to have been positive for me
Because I have learned that all of my positives
Comes from all of my negativities
The path I thought I chose for me
Was not my choice at all
It was Gods way of showing me
That without him I would fall.

LOH.LM.JH

INTRODUCTION TO WHO IS GOD

This poem is about how I went from not knowing God and into knowing and loving him. Growing up as a child I was always told by my mom and my grandma to pray to God. I prayed when I woke up, I prayed before I went to sleep, I prayed before every meal, and I also prayed for forgiveness. In the beginning, I did not know who God was, or to whom I was praying. But my grandma and my mom would always tell me that I must pray to God, and to always trust and believe in him. They said that he is my Savior. But I thought how? My life was in so much chaos, I was going through so many struggles with addictions. But they said to put my trust in him. Then I thought trust God? I have never even seen God. I could not yet feel him, or not yet hear him, but I still had to pray to him. My grandma and my mom also made sure I attended church, and in church is where I begin to know God. As I began to know him, I began to feel his presence, and it started to make me feel different on the inside. I then started going to church with my aunt. It was decades ago, but I can still remember the name of this church. It was called Faith Christian Center. I can vaguely still see the Pastor standing there in his black robe with white lace around the collar standing there preaching. I can still see me sitting there crying from the words he spoke, as they entered my soul breaking me down inside. And then at that moment I knew God was real, and I gave my life to Christ that day. So, as I was walking towards the front of the church, I cried uncontrollably. There were people there guiding me, but I also felt this presence of a big hug embracing me, but there were no arms around me, but it made me feel so warm and sentimental inside. I felt this comfort of contentment that was so beautiful, and it made me

3

feel emotional in an effective way. Then at that moment I begin to feel and hear God. Thinking back to all those days when my grandma and mom had me praying to God and going to church with my aunt, they all were preparing me to learn how to hear, feel, talk and most of all to believe in God. So now when I ask myself who is God? I can say, he is my Lord and Savior who died for my sins. He is the one who lives, works, and fights inside of me, and through all my flaws, he continues to love me unconditionally.

LOH.LM.JH

WHO IS GOD

Life was simple growing up as a kid
I did a lot of things I should not have did
I said a lot of things I should not have said
But I always prayed to God before I went to bed
I prayed not because I just wanted to
But because my grandma and mom told me to
I did not know God or who he was
But praying to him was a must
I prayed every night to this invisible being
To this supposed to be person who I was just not seeing
I prayed during the day
And I prayed in the evening
But nothing was happening for me So why do I believe in……GOD?
Growing up as a kid so vulnerable and free
There was one thing constantly installed in me
It seemed so easy but at times it was hard
Me having to pray and to always believe in God
I thought who is this God I must pray to?
And with all my heart I must believe in too.
Who is this God that I can not see
That will stop all of my pain and my miseries
Or that drug that was addicting me
Or bring back my mom and my grandma to me
I have been through so much in my life you see
So, who is this God that is supposed to save me?
Well now I can tell you who he is…..

5

Yes he is someone that I can not see
But I can feel his spirit working deep inside of me
Turning all my negatives into positivity's
As he continues to love me unconditionally
And when I am stubborn he fights inside of me
Even when I do wrong and I am guilty
He still shows me his love his grace and mercy
So who is this God that is supposed to save me?
He is my alpha he is my omega
He is my beginning and my end
From the beginning when I sinned
He still and will always love me in the end
He was tormented and tortured
He was put through agony
He died on the cross
To save a wretch like you and me
So who is the God that will save you and me?
His name is Jesus Christ, the son of God Almighty

LOH.LM.JH

INTRODUCTION TO TEMPTATION

Temptations are about the enemy in my thoughts, which had me desiring things I should not have been. As a kid I struggled with temptations. I was preyed on and victimized by them. I would try to do right, but it felt better fulfilling my temptations. It was hard fighting those desires and urges. I would just give into them, but they came with consequences. So, I had to learn how to defend them, because they were becoming contagious in my life. I would have one and then there were multiple. So, I started fighting them by fighting those crazy thoughts that the enemy was putting into my head. Knowing this is what he does, he attacks our mind, that is his battleground. But God also dwells inside of me, but he dwells more in my heart then he does in my mind. So, the more God consumed my heart, the less tempted I was in my thoughts by the enemy. I prayed for them, I fought with them, and I have even overcome them. But guess what, here comes another one along with other ones. It was hard. I love God, and no matter how much I love and trust him, till this day I still get tempted. No matter how honest and trustworthy I am, temptation is still there. No matter how much I want to do right, I'm still tempted to do wrong. As a kid it was so easy to give into my temptations. I was addicted to temptations. It was one of my hardest addictions. But now as an adult, my fight against temptations is not to think so hard on them, but to go along with my heart with constant prayer. Through prayer, being a victim of temptations becomes harder. And through love they become so much easier to face.

LOH.LM.JH

TEMPTATIONS

Everyday there is so much that I face
My good with my bad and all my mistakes
It is just love in my heart that I wish to embrace
But these temptations in me leads me to disgrace
All because what I am supposed to do for grace
I did it to please me instead
And all because what I am supposed to do for grace
I used it to get ahead
All because of my wanting thoughts
My actions became misled
And then I started doing the very things
In my life I would regret………………. My temptations…………..
My temptations started
When I was just a little kid
Doing a lot of things
My mom and grandma would forbid
And that really good life that they wanted me to live
To them I could not give
All because of those urges I had inside
Of wanting things I did not need
And all because of those urges to get it anyway
It was that feeling I had for greed
All my mom and grandma ever wanted
Was for me just to succeed
But instead I chose to hang with the crowd
Getting high and smoking weed……My temptations………………

My temptations would take over me
Each and every day
I would fight and fight with myself
Just to lead them astray
But just like the seasons they would go
But then they would come back my way
By my very own temptations
I have been betrayed
I am a victim of temptations
To temptations I am their prey
They are in my thoughts and in my mind
And inside of my body they lay
It is like resting in the bed
They rest comfortably inside of me
And they keep tempting me and tempting me
Each and every day continuously............ My temptations...............
There are these forces deep inside of me
A strong presence I can feel
I fight with them but they fight me back
Yes their existence in me are real
They come to take my joy
They come to rob and steal
I pray to my father every day for the strength
To help me make them yield
Help me to get rid of all of these distractions
And lead me into my consecration
Help me my lord to get rid of them
And to be rid of all my temptations

LOH.LM.JH

INTRODUCTION TO I AM
FIGHTING MYSELF

I am fighting myself is about me fighting me. It is about my struggle to do the right thing in the wrong situation. I struggle with these two voices in my head, the good voice, and the bad voice. My bad voice was not a voice I would hear, it was more of a negative thought that would pop into my head. But the good voice, I could always hear it loud and clear. It was my grandma's voice saying, stay strong and keep your armor on, because the devil will try to destroy you all day long. I used to be my biggest enemy. Mentally I have contradicted, and beaten myself up, all because of my discriminating thoughts against myself. I would think more about negative things in my life than I would about the positive things. My life was overwhelmed with negative things. It was those temptations I talked about in my other poem. Those urges to do what felt good, other than to do what was good. Because my thoughts would have me doing things, I know I should not have done, and had me places I knew I should not have been. Even though I had the choice to make my own decisions, my desires would sometimes take that away from me. My desires were selfish and had me making wrong decisions, holding on to grudges that I could not let go of. But as I started learning more about God, my heart began to soften. As I started following God, I started to listen more to my heart, which made it easier to block out those negative thoughts. At first it was hard, because I was confused about which voice, I was listening to. So, I stopped listening and started going along with my feelings from my heart. And through constant prayer, trusting and believing, it became easier. Easier to love those who do not love me, easier to help those who would not help me, feed, or clothe those who would not me. I now can turn the other cheek. God has control over my life, and the devil has been evicted. I now chose love over hate, by turning hate into love.

Back in the days if someone bumped into me, I was ready to fight, or I had something to say. But today if someone bumps into me, I am saying excuse me, even if it is not my fault. I have learned to respond with love from my heart, rather than reacting to those negative thoughts.

LOH.LM.JH

I AM FIGHTING MYSELF

I am fighting myself, my biggest enemy is me.
I know no one is perfect, and I know no one will be
But me, I just cannot get it right at times,
My life that is, it is just one big bind
I know I am only human, but being Godly is very tough
That line is very narrow, and the devil makes life rough
Why is it so hard to do what is right?
I beat myself up, trying to live a humble life.
Sometimes doing wrong, when I know I should do right,
With myself I fight….
It is like I have one good person on one shoulder
And a bad person on the other
One side there is influence,
The other side there is my grandmother
Influence confuses the mess out of me
Having me places I am not supposed to be
Doing things I am not supposed to do
Just to be down with the crew
Then there was my grandma saying
Always do right and do not do wrong
Always read your bible, and keep your armor on
Because the devil will try to destroy you all day long
She said it so much, it sounded like a song
Why was the question I asked myself?
Why do I let temptation take over myself?
Why cannot I just get it right with myself?

I pray to God for help.
It is not that I am a criminal,
But I am not that innocent neither
It is like at times from being good
I just need to take a breather
I always pray and I go to church
And I surely believe in God
But it is not at all that easy,
Sometimes it is just to hard
For me to forgive my enemies
When I am still hurting from what they have done to me
Or for me to turn the other cheek
When that shows signs of me being weak
Or for me to love my neighbors
But from them I cannot get any favors,
Or that it is better to give then to receive
But them people do not care that much about me
But through my faith in God I see
Myself becoming more humbly,
Being able to forgive my enemies
For all the evil they have done to me
So yes, I will turn the other cheek
No matter if I look weak
For my weakness brings me meekness
And that is what I seek.
So, I can now love my neighbors
Not looking for any favors
And I will give not looking to receive
Because my Lord made me an abler

LOH.LM.JH

INTRODUCTIONS TO THE VALLEYS MY SHIP SAILED THROUGH

My valleys are places I have been in my life. My struggles that I have faced, because of the addictions that I had. My addictions took me on many journeys, at times I was left stranded. I was locked up in jail, I was homeless and hopeless, which had me hoping for less. I had no ambition or drive to get out of that depression I was in. Even though I had the biggest support team in the world to help me (my family), I was too embarrassed to reach out. So, I went through many struggles as I sailed many ships, just trying to get to where I could fit in by doing what was right, instead of the pressure of doing wrong, just so that I can belong. The journey seemed far; I did not think I would get there, especially after experiencing hardships, going through cheating relationships, and bad friendships. I did not see that sunny day; I was just trying to find my way. And through trying to find my way I found Jesus. Jesus came and filled my life with an abundance of love and joy that I cannot explain. His love, his grace, and his mercy on me has me now forgiving and loving those who did not forgive or love me, because that is what God has done for me. So now as I worship him my life has been on a spaceship soaring ever since, soaring into healthy relationships, soaring into leadership. Soaring into all of the wonderfulness of his lordship. Please enjoy this poem, it is my journey on the battleship.

LOH.LM.JH

THE VALLEYS MY SHIP BEEN THROUGH

Almighty God, creator of this world
The maker of all things, created a little girl
He sent her through many valleys
As she sailed so many ships
Some good some bad relationships
And also some broken friendships
Some days when her ship sailed,
Underneath there was no water
There was no deck for her ship to dock
Her ship at times out of order
She had hardship turning into warship
And she faced so many battles
Just looking for good companionship
She had to sail so many travels
She did not know she needed a membership
Just so that she can belong
So she went through an internship
Of doing everything wrong
At times her ship was stranded
She had no gas to make it through
She had no shelter to keep her from the storms
But then worship brought her through
Worship took her to a spaceship
Where she then begin to soar

Soaring into Lordship
As she began to Love the Lord
Going through an apprenticeship
Receiving a scholarship for loving the Lord
Now all her hardship and warship
All of them are no more
Now she focuses on leadership
Learning from the valleys her ship sailed through
Taking home a championship
Because her God has brought her through

LOH.LM.JH

INTRODUCTION TO
HOW DO I BELIEVE

How do I believe is about the testing of my faith. I did not understand how I was supposed to believe in God when there was so much negativity going on in the world. I was struggling, I was struggling in an abusive relationship, struggling with addictions. I could not tell right from wrong, because in my mind I felt like my wrongs were rightly justified, and my rights were right. Not that I could not tell the difference, but it really did not matter. Back then in my life, survival is what mattered. That is what I fought for every day, to survive. However, I could in a world full of backstabbers, liars, thieves, and cheaters. People with no respect or morals for others. People that worried about getting that fast money however they could without being disrespected. That is what I knew. That is where my comfort zone was. I did not even know how to relate to people outside of that type of circle. But one day a friend and I decided that we were going to start church hopping so that we could find us a church. So, the first Sunday we went to this big and beautiful church. The choir sung and it was ok, and then the pastor came out to preach but it was not effective to me. So, the next Sunday we went to a different church, it was a store front type of church. So, as we went in, the choir was singing. It was a much smaller choir than the church we went to the Sunday before, but their music had more of a blessing on my soul. Then the Pastor came out and started preaching. I mind you I was already feeling a little sentimental and emotional inside from the choir. So, when the Pastor started preaching, I began to feel unfamiliar inside and a little bit confused, because this pastor was preaching my

17

whole life right there on stage. I could not believe it; my life story was his message. I started looking around to see if anyone was looking like how I was feeling. I then started getting increasingly emotional as he spoke, and I just wanted to explode. I could not understand it, how did he know my struggles? And at that moment I realized it was God speaking to me through him. God used the pastor to speak to me sending me a personal shout out to let me know that he was still there working for me and working inside of me. So, me not being able to hold it all inside anymore, I begin to scream, and I cried out to God. I then began to feel his presence, and I heard him say STEP BACK, I AM IN CONTROL!! And once again I gave my life to Christ. This time it has been more effective for me because I now let God take the lead. Do not get me wrong I still will try to take the lead at times, but that is when God whispers to me that he is in control.

LOH.LM.JH

HOW DO I BELIEVE

How do I believe
In something I cannot see
When there is all of this pain, frustration
And unfairness around me
There are so many people out there struggling
And their hungry kids are crying
Dealing with a global pandemic
That had so many people out there dying
My life was such a struggle, growing up in the hood
I was molested as a child, and my boyfriend was no good
I was a teen hooked on drugs
I could not tell right from wrong
Because I thought the way I was living was fine
But truthfully I was gone
I was stuck in the wilderness around a lot of lost people
I couldn't really help myself being around so much evil
But the strange thing about it, to me it felt good
Being around those lost people
And stuck in the hood
Because there I felt like I belonged
I was comfortable in my surroundings
I was settled and content
And I was living in my own boundaries
I was actually to scared

To step out of my comfort zone
And leaving what was familiar to me
Because my back had no bone
I thought if I stepped out I would be a failure you see
I thought that there was nothing out there better for me
At times I felt like I was less then you see
I would then cry out but no one would hear me
But then one day a friend invited me to church
And it totally blew me away
Because the pastor was preaching
On my life that day
This man knew nothing about my life nor me
But his every word he spoke was identifying me
It was like he knew me inside and out
I then began to cry, scream and I shout
Then I heard God speaking to me
And he said that was not your life
And that he had a purpose for me
So then he put on my heart
Abundance, love, and joy
He said if you step out on faith for me
All of this is yours
Then something inside of me started feeling strange
And at that very moment I felt my life change
I then began to pray and I asked God why?
Why all of the hardship in the wilderness?
And his answer made me cry
He said my child my love is unconditional for you
And I give you free will to do what you want to do
When you are taking control
And trying to run your own life

Life is much harder
And filled with much strife
But when you step back and let me take charge
Things will become easier they will no longer be hard
So on that very day
I stepped into the house of the lord
I have now learned to love
And appreciate him more
So I ask myself now how do I believe
I believe in him because he first believed in me

LOH.LM.JH

INTRODUCTION TO WHAT IS LIFE

What is life is about life, and my perspective of how I seen life. I grew up seeing life one way, but it turned out to be a whole totally different way. When I grew up and started living on my own, life became more of an everyday struggle for me. I struggled trying to deal with difficult people in my life. I struggled to be consistent with my daily activities such as going to work and dealing with my addictions. On top of that, trying to make enough money to pay my bills and support my addictions at the same time. I was getting paid every two weeks, trying to make enough money to pay the same bills every month, dealing with the same struggles every day. Repeating the same thing over and over each and everyday, it was driving me crazy. I know I had to pay my bills so that I could have a roof over my head and food to eat, but I was stressing to live life. Stressing in my relationship with an abusive cheater who tried to convince me that I was the cheater. But this is who I chose to love, someone who made me feel that being disrespectful to me was some form of love, even though it made me feel insecure and intimidated. That was not living life, but that was my life. I needed an out, my mind needed something other than my relationship or a constant worry about how my bills would get paid. But this was the path I chose for myself, yes, I could of made better choices, but I didn't, so what do I do? Now I put more of my trust, and my faith into God, because he has brought me a long way. I did not see myself here where I am now, but God did, because he never gave up on me. He brought me to where I am, and he continues to bless me by taking me further. God is first in my life, he helps me to look and I move forward as I learn from where I have been. I now see life so much differently. I do not take life for granted anymore. I take life as a breath of fresh air, being able to breathe the air that God has given to me, because when that breath of air is gone, so is my life here on earth. So, I do not stress over life, I show love and I live it. That is what God wants us to do. He is our stress reliever.

LOH.LM.JH

WHAT IS LIFE?

Is life just waking up in the morning
After a nighttime of sleep
Is life just working to make that money
For clothes to wear or food to eat
Life is not supposed to be a struggle
Even though we do it somedays
Struggling not to dispute with someone
Because it is just not going our way
Struggling because you know you are right
But they are saying that you are wrong
Struggling not to fight over it
Instead letting it go and move on
We have been misinformed about life
By humans who give out misinformation
They have you believing that your life you live
It is only just an equation
Of waking up, working, and going back to bed
But is that really life?
Dealing with people's bitterness
Their anger and their strife
Having lusting feelings for people or things
Lusting over your husband or your wife
That is not life!!
Life to me is being able to take a breath of fresh air
And in each inhale that I take I feel the beauty of love

And there is nothing but God that I fear
I do not gasp for it, I just breathe it......
Do you feel that life?

Life is God we all have him
I know because he lives inside of me
But at times I did not live outside for him
I was dwelling in misery
Life...... what is life?
Life is that hope or that fantasy that comes true
Life is that melody that melts my heart
And bring tears to my eyes, I'm blue
Life is a still blue sky over a calm sea
Arising is the sun
Life is knowing when life is over there is life
The everlasting one
I used to be in very dark places chasing very dark things
Just to feel good for that moment
Not knowing it was just a temporary feeling
But I still kept on hoping
So I just kept on chasing, chasing a feeling, chasing a high
Chasing a man or a women
Chasing after people and things
That I should have been running from in the beginning
Living life for me used to be a job
I got my experience from living life
Learning people's personalities and attitudes
I see now why peoples life is filled with strife
But that is not life....

Whatever is a part of your life you feed it
If not, you or it will starve

So do not feed your anger or bad habits
Try feeding you Holy Spirit, your God
Why do you even feed your bad habits
When that is something you are bad at
Why feed addiction or anger
Why not try starving that

LOH.LM.JH

INTRODUCTION TO FAITH

This poem is about how I chose to use my faith. What is faith? It is to have complete trust and confidence in something or someone. Now, we all have faith in something or someone, even if or when they or it fails us. Sometimes we choose to have faith in people who disappoint us, or sometimes we may choose to have faith in our car that breaks down on us. We do not know why we put our faith into things that let us down, but we do. Me I used to, but now I put my faith into God. I do not put my faith into people, I put my faith into God to help me to deal with people. I do not put my faith into the car, I put my faith into God to keep me safe while I am inside of the vehicle, and for resources of help if I should break down. Putting my faith more into God then I do in people, it guarantees me to be ok, I do not ever have to worry about God letting me down or breaking down on me. Through my faith in him I have learned to love, I have learned to love difficult people, people who need forgiveness, just like me. I now choose love over hate, even when I am not receiving love in return. It does not help me to hate. God wants me to love in all situations, whether good or bad. I try hard to do it, but it is not easy. Especially if you are dealing with racism, domestic, sexual or any type of abuse. It is not easy to love them. Sometimes I have to take myself outside of the box in order to forgive abusers. Even though I have not abused anyone, I have done things in my life that I needed and still need forgiveness for. And God forgives me, always and unconditionally. Sometimes I have to take the time to put myself into other people's shoes, because I use to wear their shoes.

LOH.LM.JH

FAITH

When you trust and believe in something our someone
That is called FAITH!!
When you dislike someone because of race, color, or gender
That is called HATE!!
Everyone has faith in something or someone,
Because we all receive faith from the father and the son
Together with the Holy Spirit, they live inside us as one
But do you ever look inside of yourself and never see NONE?
How do you use your Faith…..?

Do you put your faith into disliking someone
Because you feel that they are unworthy of
Or do you put your faith into treating all people equal
And showing everyone the same love
Why is it we see some people different
Is it because we feel indifferent
Or is it because of peoples who's generational curse
Is just to be ignorant
So is that supposed to make you or I ignorant
No, I choose not to be
I choose to use my faith to love everyone
Even if everyone does not love me
Yes, it is hard to love someone
Who is filled with hate and negativity
Who hates me just because of the color of my skin
Even though they physically do not know me

But my love for people who hate
That is bigger than you and me
And for me to judge or dislike someone
That is just not up to me
All my life the color of people's skin
It has always been at a debate
And I have been thrown shade, because of my shade
By people filled with so much hate
To have all types of people on this earth
Do you think anyone is a mistake
How can anyone take the authority
To use their faith to discriminate
They put more energy into hating someone
Instead of showing that person some love
At the end of the day whatever happen, it happened
We cannot take it back, yes life is rough
But Faith…..

Faith is that feeling that you put your trust into
To do what is right and to be obedient
Even though as it is breaking you down inside
You trust it as your heart becomes lenient
And even though it may break you down
Once or twice again
When you rely, believe, and trust in your faith
You know in your heart it will be alright in the end

Hate will not change anything, but love will give us equality
Love and treat everyone the same and it will become a reality

LOH.LM.JH

INTRODUCTION TO
WHAT IS LOVE

Growing up as children, we learn how to love through our families. Then as we get older, we have friends or relationships we may show our love to. But just because we may love someone, that does not mean that we are receiving love in return. Sometimes loving others blinds us, that we feel love even through abuse, guilt, insecurities, etc. I am an emotional person, and I use to love easily. But I have learned that everyone does not love the same. Just trying to find that person who would be there for you like your family would be, was challenging. I would always be there ready to help, but when I needed it, there were just a few that would be there. Love is not one sided, and love is not giving up in challenging times. Love is making it work together, through ups and downs and through in and outs. Love is Unconditional..... NO, conditions!!

LOH.LM.JH

WHAT IS LOVE?

What is love?

Is it what someone can do for you?
Or is it what they do for you?
Is it when they tell you what you want to hear?
Or is it the truth that is told that you do not want to hear?
Is it how they make you feel?
Or is it how you would like to feel?

REAL LOVE

When love is given,
It comes from that person heart
It is not the money that they put into it,
It is the time that they put into the art
It is not for show or competition
It is not for you just to bare
It is to show affection, truth, and respect
It is to show that you truly care
Telling someone that you love them all day
But stabbing them in the back at night
Kissing, hugging, and making love
Right after a serious fight
Because of all of the dirt you done in the dark
It has now come into the light
Apologizing when you are wrong

That does not make it right
Love is being honest with yourself first
And admitting when you are wrong
Love will then kick in the remorse
To continue to make your love strong
Love is not when tough times hit
And you are giving up saying I'm done
Love is when you work out those hard times
Happily, together as one.

LOH.LM.JH

MY DAILY BREAD

My daily bread is not food that I eat,
My daily bread is not vegetables nor meat
My daily bread is the love I get from God
And without it my day is incomplete
My daily bread is the word from God
That helps pushes me towards my goals
My daily bread is more than food for hunger
It is food that feeds my soul
My daily bread it encourages me
It also gives me strength
When I go through my hard days
I can face each consequence
I need it every morning
And I need it every night
I need it all during my day
Because of the enemy who I fight
I am hungrier for my daily bread
Then I am for food to eat
I will fast all month on my daily bread
Defending the enemy who tries to defeat
He tries to defeat me out of my purpose
He tries to defeat me out of my inheritance
But defeating me he cannot,
Because to me he is just irrelevant
He tries to take my happiness
And he tries to take my joy

He tries to take everything that I love
As he also tries to destroy
But when I get my daily bread
I throw a scripture at that imposter
Isaiah 54:17
No weapon formed against me shall prosper
He pops in my thoughts telling me I can not do it
His battleground is in my head you see
But then I hit him with Philippians 4:13
I can do all things through Christ who strengthens me
When I get my daily bread, the enemy becomes unclever
Because Isaiah 40:8 says that the word of God endures forever

LOH.LM.JH

THE HYPOCRITE IN ME

I am frustrated at me, for being frustrated at you
I'm always complaining about all of the wrong that you do
What is so frustrating about it, is that what you do
I am also guilty of doing it too
It may not be to the extreme that you do
It may not be as much as you do
But who am I to criticize you
When me doing it means, I am just as wrong as you
I am blind to my wrong doings, it is easier to see yours
It is easier to point the finger at you, that is just my choice
I know it is selfish of me, and it dose not make it right
Me complaining about a lie you told, that I just told last night
I tell you not to hate, and to always show people love
But when you ask me if I love all people, my answer is sort of
Ask me do I care for all people; I will say nah I think not
But when you said that you hate your moms
I am judging you straight off top.
Because I cannot see no one hating on their mom
Or any family member at that
But that dude that violates other people
Yeah, I hate that cat

Hate is hate, and a lie is a lie
Stealing is stealing, and getting high is getting high
Why do we sugarcoat things when it is done by us
But when it is someone else doing it, we just love to fuss

LOH.LM.JH

JUDGING

There are people in this world, who live miserable lives
They had awful up bringing's, and they struggled to survive
They faced additions, molestation, and they have been abused
They have been convicted and called liars, and also been misused
These people they grow up with this anger inside
Their struggles are real because they have not, no pride
They are the underdogs, with no silver spoons in their mouths
They are just maintaining and surviving as they are roughing it out
Robbing, lying and cheating, doing what they must do
To stay above water, but folks do not know what they are going through
But they are so easily judged…..

WHO ARE YOU TO JUDGE?

Why would you judge me for the wrong that I do
Are you perfect, how would you like it if I judged you
Yes, I am a person, who is in love with the same gender
But to the same almighty God my heart I surrender
But people like to judge me, because of who I am
But please answer a question, do those people not sin
Or are they already perfect from beginning until the end
So why treat people in an indifferent way
When to the same Almighty God all of us pray
Let God be the judge, for he will have the last say
Of which he will on judgement day
So, do not look at me in any different way

All I ask from you for me is to pray
And I will do the same for you till my life on earth end
And that is pray for you and forgiveness of your sins

People in this world love to judge. They will judge you on your looks, how you act, your race, what you do, and I can go on and on about how people judge. I may even get judged for my book. But that is neither here nor there for me because at the end of the day, the only judgements about me that matters are Gods and mine, and God dose not judge. So, I am not thinking about people's thoughts and outlook of me, I'm thinking about Gods outlook of me. Most of my life the way people felt about me, the things they said about me, and the way they thought about me was important to me. Till this day, I do not understand why that was so important to me. Because trying to figure out other people's thoughts and opinions about me was stressful. Until I realized that it was only my opinion that counted anyway.

Trust in yourself!!

BELIEVE IN YOURSELF NOT SOMEONE ELSE IN YOU!!

LOH.LM.JH

DEDICATED
MY LIFE TO YOU

I have come to far in my life lord
Not to be committed to you
With all my faults that I have Lord
You still brought me through
I am a sinner Lord
Who you continuously show your love to
So I am dedicating my life Lord, I have dedicated it to you

I have been hurt committing my life to others
And I have been hurt trusting in them too
I have been neglected by them and abused by them
Because I was dedicated to them and not you
But now my heart it beats for you Lord
My life I now live for you too
My thoughts are more on the life you have for me
So I am dedicating my life to you

You came to give me eternal life
A better life than I could ever imagine Lord
So you sacrificed your life just for me
Sustaining thirty-nine lashes Lord

You have done so much more for me
Then anyone in my life will ever do
That is why I am dedicating my life to you Lord
I have dedicated it to you

LOH.LM.JH

GIVING THANKS

Today is the day that I give thanks
For all my blessings from above
Today is the day I raise my hands
To thank him for giving me love
I am a planted seed, planted by God
To do my absolute best
He reigns on me with nothing but love
And now my harvest manifests
I am reaping what I sowed
And now I sow nothing but love
But even if I do any wrong
His still gives me his Godly love
I want to thank you God
Thank you for your comfort
Thank you for the sins in my life
Through you I have triumphant
Looking back on where I came from
I did not think there were brighter days ahead
God, I know without you in my life
I probably would be dead
So my heart will continue to cry for you
And longing for one of your hugs
As my body forever urges for you
And your unconditional love

LOH.LM.JH

I AM A FEIN

I am a recovering addict
I have recovered from some hard drugs
Crack cocaine, marijuana
And some other things I can think of
My mind would only think of it
And my body always urged for it
My days constantly consisted of it
Yes, I was a Fein for it
No longer do I consume it
It is no longer in my mix
There is something new that I Fein for, I have a new fix
And when I wake up in the morning, I need my new fix
I Fein for it, I want it, I am a junkie for it
I fall on my knees and I nod for it
I get the trembles and the shakes, I cry out for it
I am a Fein……….

What is my drug of choice?
It is my love for the Lord, through him I am rejoiced
If the Lord was a drug, I'll stay high on him everyday
When I want a dose, all I have to do is pray
I am a Fein………

Please bring me my cord
Wrap it around my arm and shoot me up with the Lord
I want him in my veins, and make my pupils dilate

I want him flowing through my blood, speeding up my heart rate
I am a Fein……….

If the Lord was a drink, I will have shots all day
You will think I am drunk like Hannah in 1Samuel 1:13
Praying with my heart, with a mumble from my mouth
Lips are moving, but nothing is coming out
I am a Fein…..

I need him everyday
I don't need to detox, and withdrawals go away
God is the best high ever, I'll O.D. everyday
On my love for the Lord, who is making my way I am a Fein…..

I have been diagnosed
That I am a Fein for the father, the son and the holy ghost
For they are my urge, and for them I will boast
Ill go find them wherever I have to, I will travel coast to coast
I am a Fein…..

LOH.LM.JH

NARCOTIC ANONYMOUS

When you hear the letters N A
You think of Narcotic Anonymous
It is a place where people go to speak out their feelings
It is like speaking to a group of psychologists
I once was a member of Narcotic Anonymous
And that is what the letters N A meant to me
But after getting those tokens, and taking it one day at a time
N A has become so many other meanings
My N A does not just stand for Narcotic Anonymous,
It stands for NOT ANYMORE!!
It is me taking a stand in my life
And standing for what I live for
It stands for NO ABUSE!!
I love myself and I will not abuse myself again
Any friends, people, or domestic abuse
In my life has come to an end
It stands for NEED ANYTHING!!
I received so many numbers and hugs
They said call me if you need anything
Especially before the need to use drugs
It stands for NEVER AGAIN!!
Even though I tell myself to never say never everyday
But saying I will never do it again becomes easier
With the help of all of my N A's
It stands for my NEW ATTITUDE!!
That is what N A has given to me

I have been addicted to so many ugly things
But now I am addicted to the love in me
It stands for NO AMATEUR!!
Professional in me I see
And it stands for my NEW APPRECIATION in my life
And for all the love God has given to me.

LOH.LM.JH

INSPIRED DRUG DEALER

All my life growing up as a kid
I thought about who I would be
I thought about me being rich
Living in a nice big house with my family
I was a lost child growing up in the hood
Someone just trying to find her way
I was seeing those struggles of determine people
Fighting to go to work each and everyday
They were out there struggling and working so hard
Bodies worn down because of old age
Breaking their backs to do their jobs
Just to take home that minimum wage
But I did not see that for my life
Nah that was not my plan for me
My plans were to become the biggest drug dealer
Because they were my role model you see
I seen my house, my cars and lots of money
All coming to me at a fast rate
Not knowing the drug dealer dealing drugs
Would soon become a drug intake
Then I started blowing that fast money that I would make
Waking up every morning to wake an bake
Me an inspired rich drug dealer
I was just a fake
Yes, I thought I could make a career
Out of being the biggest drug dealer

But it landed me locked up behind bars
And my life became so much realer
I thought my life would be so easy
But it turned out to be so hard
Still trying to get that fast money
But it came to me even harder
Looking back now on my role model
A drug dealer was not so inspiring at all
It took me absolutely no where positive
It took me to the very places that made me fall
So I snapped out of the thought of becoming a
drug dealer
After being paroled for fifteen years
Knowing if I would ever go back
That the penitentiary would be my career.

LOH.LM.JH

EMOTIONAL

I am an emotional person
Who gives up all of me
At times my emotions blind me
And I just cannot see
Sometimes my emotions hurt me
Because my heart gets in the way
Sometimes my emotions fool me
Because a game on me they play
Emotions to me are personal
At least that is what I thought
Until you share them with other people
And in others your emotions are caught
They get caught into friends who will play with them
And your loved one might do the same
Your family will try to take care of them
Because they feel your pain
Why do we even need emotions
To love, to hate, or to be happy, or sad
Why can't we just take the good with the bad
Because sometimes I do not want to laugh
And sometimes I do not want to cry
All because one lives
Or all because one dies
Sometimes I wish I was water
Just flowing along the stream
Sometimes I wish I was a tree with leaves

Just blowing along with the breeze
Sometimes I wish I was a bird
Soaring high up into the sky
Sometimes I wish I did not have to worry
If the truth is really a lie
I just don't want to feel sometimes
That is just how I choose to be
Sometimes I wish that I can just be
Emotionally Free

LOH.LM.JH

STANDING BEHIND THE CROSS

I try spending my days, standing behind the cross
Because the day I get in front of it, in that day I am lost
I be lost and confused, and I cannot find my way
But with the cross leading in front of me, all I have to do is pray
I pray to the cross for my problems
And I leave them on the throne
My life is dedicated to the cross
Because my life is not my own
The cross is my shield, and it give to me protection
The cross is my guide, it shows to me directions
The cross is my teacher, it teaches me my lessons
The cross is my God, who gives to me my blessings
There behind the cross, I feel so relentless
The magnitude of my life, it is greatly immenseness
When I am behind the cross, I am whatever I want to be
Because behind the cross
I can do all things through Christ who strengthens me
There behind the cross, it is so calm and soothing there
I can feel the love of God in my soul
That my heart start crying tears
Tears that are full of love and joy
That makes my heart feel warm inside
I never thought I would feel love in my heart
That comes just from a cry
So, if you are ever looking, and you want to find me

Look behind the cross, because that is where I will be
I will be there getting my blessings
From the cross that is my guard
I will be there praising and worshipping
And giving love to my awesome God

LOH.LM.JH

STANDING OUT IN THE CROWD

You have a voice inside,
Please do not hide it
If someone takes offense towards you,
Do not be ashamed take pride in it
Hold your head up high
And put some stride in it
Because truthfully in the end
You are the ones who is providing it
Just like yours,
my life I would die for it
And just like I do deep in my heart
I sometimes cry for it
It gets lonely out there
With just you alone
So, we sometimes go along with peoples reality
Instead of going along with our own
We go along with friends
Instead of dealing with our own beings
Because friends will try to break you down
Just for the purpose they are seeing
But my pride in me says don't stop, just watch
Watch as I go high as the clouds
Watch how I just keep on soaring
To make my grandma and mom proud
I just want to love and be positive
There is no more negativity in me allowed

Because I do not want to be lost anymore
I want to stand out in the crowd
I want to be unique
I want to be me
I want to be who
God has made me to be
Now in my life and throughout eternity
Because looking back that journey
Has been long and hard for me
Some of my friends has gone
And a couple are still here with me
But God and my family continues
To always be there for me

LOH.LM.JH

A POEM FOR MY GRANDMA

Grandma my love I truly miss you
I miss all that you say, and all that you do
I missed those times that we laughed
I miss the times that we cried
But there is one thing grandma I do not miss
And that is telling you goodbye
You know growing up as a child grandma
I took a lot for granted
Not realizing how deeply
Your love for me was planted
To me I was just a seed
Deep inside of the dirt
Not realizing how my actions
Sometimes made you hurt
But you continued to give me water
Those words of wisdom that you know
And then out of the dirt grandma
I then began to grow
Yes some petals did fall
And some branches they did break
But that stem that you planted grandma
It is still standing up straight
Now I am a full flower
And up to you I sing
Thank you my dear grandma
For spreading on me your wings

Ever since I was a child
And even now as a matured lady
I want to say how much I love you
And thank you for all of the love you gave me
So, I am sending you this message
With a very big hug
With lots and lots and lots of kisses
Along with all of my love

LOH.LM.JH

A POEM FOR MY MOM

Mommy I truly miss you
Not being here with me
I thought together here on earth
We'd be together always as a family
I remember growing up,
It was you, me, and my two brothers
Even though we did not have that much
We always had each other
Mommy as a single parent
You sometimes struggled to make it through
But nobody would ever know it
Because you kept us looking brand new
And even though at times money was tight
Mommy you would never skip a beat
When it came to putting clothes on our back
Or when it came to food to eat
You taught us to be respectful
And to always be mindful of other
And to never ever break the code of love
Between your sister and your brothers
And she would never ever break the code of love
Between her daughter and her sons
She loved us everyday of our lives
Together we were one
I remember you making Christmas time seeming like a fantasy
Because we had so much love under the Christmas tree

With so much joy and love all around us
You made this a special day for me
Because it did not matter how much we had
And it did not matter where we lived
Christmas time was always about
The mothers love to her child she gives
Her love for us was genuine
And I miss that so much
But even on the other side mommy
Our hearts you will always touch
Mommy I really miss you
I wish you were here with me
Because I am missing your motherly love
That you have always given to me
I miss you calling my name
And I miss your beautiful smile
I just want to go back mommy
To being my mothers child
I want to go back in my life
Where you kept me away from harm
I just want to go back mommy
To you holding me in your arms

LOH.LM.JH

BLAME IT ON ME

Blame it on you do not blame it on me
Do not blame it on Adam and do not blame it on Eve
Do not blame it on anyone if you fall
Do not even blame it on the alcohol
Because the choices in life is what you make
And those steps in life is what you take
So when you reach the golden gate
You can only blame you for the outcome of your fate

LOH.LM.JH

FORGIVENESS

I have this passionate feeling that dwells inside of me
Ever since I have been back into church
At times it brings tears to my eyes
As it consoles all my hurts
And every time I feel or talk about it
I feel this presence of a really strong bond
This feeling and who I am talking about
It is all about my God
I feel his love so abundantly
Each and every day
It lets me know through my faith in him
That things will be ok
His love, his grace, and his mercy for me
Helps me to have love for all things
And also to have love for all people
Because of the love he shows and brings
These feelings that I have received from God
Helps me to see things in a different view
I can now forgive which was hard for me
Because if someone hurt me, I had to hurt them back too
But when God told me I was supposed to forgive
My question to him was why?
He told me that forgiveness was healing for me
So I said yes I will give it a try
Because I would always dwell on things
That people have done to me

But God said let it go and forgive
And then my soul shall be free
So I pondered on all of my mistakes
And how God has always forgiven me
So I had to forgive, in order to move on
And stop that dwelling in my miseries
Because I was just making a hypocrite of myself
Because people I have also hurt
But God took my hurts and turned them into love
Now my thoughts and my heart he converts

LOH.LM.JH

INNOCENSE GONE

Hey look at that brand new baby
Born into this world
She is so beautiful chunky and jolly
It is mommy and daddy's little girl
Her mind is free of worries
And her soul is free of sins
She looks up at her parents smiling
Because on them she depends
But as she gets older
She starts finding her on way
That is when her mind free worries and soul free sins
Are starting to fade away
She is feeling confused
In a world full of so many choices
Mom and grandma in one ear, friends in other
In her head there are so many voices
She struggles with which voices she should listen to
So she goes with what makes her feel good
It does not matter if she goes right or wrong
Either way she will be misunderstood
Getting more motivation from her friends
She rebels the voices of her family
Because with her family she had to follow rules
But with her friends she could be free
But everyone's goal was the same for her
It was to get that money and to be a success

But to her, it did not matter how she got it
So she thought the fast way would be best

GETTING THAT MONEY

She thought that money would be the answer, to all of her problems
She thought that the money would help her to solve them
So she started grinding, stacking money was her goal
She did what she had to do to get, even tarnishing her soul
She was out there slinging, trying to get paid
She started getting high, door kicked in in a police raid
Her life then got crazy, trying to maintain her role
Getting high off her product, smoking up her goals
It made her think back to the voice she chose to listen to
It made her want to go back to change those choices too
But thanks to God for sending Jesus to burden her sins
And giving her the chance to start all over again.

LOH.LM.JH

NO MORE STRESS

I woke up this morning with my mind feeling cluttered
Thinking about in my life what to do next
It is another morning but it still feels like yesterday
And I am feeling a little perplexed
As I get my day started all the stress from the past weeks
In my mind starts to resurface
But I'm stressing with myself to get through the next weeks
And staying focused each day on my purpose
My heart is always in it for my purpose
But my thoughts they think a little different.
It is like as my thoughts speak to my heart
My thoughts will become belligerent
My thoughts be fighting with my heart
Because it is my heart I want to give into
Because my thoughts will be having me stressing and struggling
And fighting each day for my mental
Oh how a ride on the highway
Helps me to relieve so much stress
My windows are cracked, blowing one in the air
As I am inhaling very deep breaths
As my mind starts to focus, it becomes more clearer
As it wonders up into the clouds
Eyes are tightening, trees in the rear view fading
While my mind is dancing to musical sounds
I take another drag on that gas as I step harder on the gas
Now my car feels like it is gliding

Doing ninety miles and hour wind hitting my face
It is cloud nine I find myself riding
As I'm on cloud nine on the expressway,
My mind it begins to express
How right now I am feeling like I have no cares in the world
And definitely no more stress

LOH.LM.JH

UNJUSTIFIED

Hands up I can not breathe,
Are you death and blind and can not see
You just murdered that unarmed man right in front of me,
And the judge let you go free how can this be?
Can someone please explain to me
How is this world revolving?
You know with all of these political issues
And all of the black and blue problems
Can you tell me who will solve them?

Is it those judges who judge black people cases,
The ones who give out lesser time to most of the white faces
Who gives free get out of jail cards, for our murdered lives wasted
To those cops who came in, invading our spaces
They came in flexing their guns and their tasers,
We can see all of the facts, but we can not call it races
So now you all worried about the riots in your cities,
And trust me I get it
But do you understand
Just what it is we deal with?
From the beatings and hangings in slavery,
To now killing our unarmed Black men
While we wait months to get a verdict,
We have tried the peaceful protesting
But then you come with these bogus verdicts,
Thinking we are dumb and unaware

You be giving out innocent pleas,
When being guilty was absolutely clear
You be letting them go free, this is our fear
It is like a spit in our face, because truthfully you don't care
This is why we react by rioting, we are like time bombs inside
Dealing with all of the unfairness, we have dealt with all of our lives
Seeing the deaths of Breanna Taylor, George Floyd and all the others,
This makes me angry inside
But your focus is more on the rioting,
What about how they died?
We are so tired of having to compete, when it will only turn into defeat
And it is not because you won, it is because you are a liar and a cheat
This is a messed-up way we are treated, and those good politics you do
speak it
Because when it comes between you and us, we are just deleted
Can someone explain to me, why are we treated differently?
When we are all humans that were born with a brain and a heart,
We all have thoughts and feelings,
That was given to us from the start
We all are given hands to feel, and we all have eyes to see
So tell me what do you see, that is different in me
Besides a human being with a different personality,
Different flavors different cultures, THIS IS REALITY!!
So face it all of you hypocrites and races,
Who hide your faces behind badges and unjustified cases
You promote all of this hatred and all of those paces
Up and down the streets because of our innocent lives wasted
So tell me when will you taste it, and not just haste it?
When will you feel it, and not just waste it?
When will you face it, and not just caste it?
When will we have justice, so that we can embrace it?

LOH.LM.JH

SLAVE MENTALITY

A Slave
A person made to do exhausting labor with restricted freedom.
To be in bondage
To be servitude
To be in subjugation
Humans made to serve Humans.

So…. can I lay some knowledge on you?
From 1619 to 1863
Because of being black, our ancestors were in slavery
They were molested, raped, beaten, tortured, and hung,
It did not matter how old they were, and it did not matter how young
They were terrified, petrified, and they were made to live fearful
They were horrified, frightened, and they were killed if not careful.
And me knowing all of this, it makes my heart ache
It makes my heart heavy, that it makes my heart break
Because now in the 20th century, when all of us are free
Some of our minds are still locked up into that slave mentality
Why do we still blame them folks for what happened decades ago
Why cannot we move on, and just let it go
Our ancestors were the ones afflicted, but we still carry the bitterness
They went through the agony, but we are the ones lost in dispiritedness
Why do we feel we are owed something? Face it we are all free
It is time we start doing our own thing, and unlock that slave mentality
Cause no matter how much we feel they owe us, a feeling is all it will be
Because if we do not go out, earn and get it

That is something we will never see
Do not let our ancestors look down on us now
And see that we are taking freedom as just being free
Let us get up and go be the go getters
That our ancestors expects us to be
We be out here wasting our hard earned money
On things like platinum and gold chains
We are out here making these people rich just to feel sustained
Tell me did our ancestors feel sustained?
While they were out there on the chain gang
At one wrong move
They were at a risk of being hanged
They were forced to work for free
They had no income from their jobs
But now that we can make the income
We feel like working for it is too hard
We are too impatient on making that slow money
We would rather make that fast money illegally
Then you would be locked back up in chains and bars
And once again, a slave mentally
And why do we take our hard-earned money
And we spend it on envying stuff
Instead of us investing in our own businesses
So that we can envy ourselves
But no, we are more focused on impressing someone
On our looks or what we have
Instead of our minds being Knowledgeable
Bragging about how many certifications we have
We are feeding right into their hand
To be free with stupidity
Because yes, we may have some money
But do we have any equity
Instead of taking our hard-earned money

And investing it in buying acres of land
We spend all our money getting tatted all up
And that is a symbol of being brand
But that is what makes our esteem high
It is the Tats, the Platinum, and the Gold
We are idolizing all of this stuff
But we are broken in our souls
That is why I ask you my people
What are you doing with your bread?
Do you know that the devils battle ground?
It Is right here in our heads
We be out here robbing and stealing from one another.
And stabbing each other in the back
I tell you our problem is not just black and white
Sometimes our problems are blacks on blacks.
Look we are already being discriminated against
Then to be discriminated by each other
Even though in reality
We are all supposed to be sisters and brothers
Black minds together are a powerful thing
Black minds separated is a dangerous thing
So lets build our nationality up together
So we will can make our nation ring

LOH.LM.JH

I WANT TO MEET YOUR SPIRIT

I do not want to meet you as a person
I want to meet your spirit instead
Because at times when I meet people personally
Sometimes I just feel misled
I have met a lot of people in my life
That portray this beautiful sight
They tell you everything that you want to hear
But their aura is just not right
But when I feel you spiritually
There is this connection that comes over me
Connecting me right through to your heart
Because your spirit is consoling me
It is the spirit that is in each one of us
It is the spirit of Jesus Christ
To us all he has given the Holy Spirit
And for that he has paid the price
He paid the price for this love
For all of us to receive
He paid it for us with his life
Right there on calvary
So do not frown when I meet you
Because I will greet you with a smile
I will greet you with my love inside
Like a mother greets her child
So can I meet you spiritually
I want to meet the Jesus in you

I want to meet your positive side
Because your negative side will not do
So there is no need to say I love you
Because those words are easy to say
Just show to me your spiritual love
And that is where my heart will lay
So can I meet the Jesus in you
I am not trying to meet no one else
Because for my family, friends, and people in my path
I will give my spiritual self
I want to meet the Jesus in you
Because you can't love me if you do not love yourself
So can I meet the Jesus in you
I am not trying to meet no one else
Because I have met so many different people in my life
With so many different personalities
Some of them good hearted, some of them hateful
Which brought me to reality
That we may look a little different
But we are all Gods people
And from my spirit to your spirit
We are all created equal
So I want to meet the Jesus in you
That love that everyone sees
And my love to you I will show
Along with the Jesus in me

LOH.LM.JH

I FORGIVE

You abuser and user you took away the innocence from the innocent
And now their innocence is gone
Why would you do this? Is it just for a minute of pleasure?
But for a lifetime their innocence is torn
Their deep inner thoughts about you
It is hard to bare and they can not move on
Even though it is many years later
When the presence of you is gone
I am so mad at you
Because of what you did
Someone that was looked up to
And someone their family trusted
But because of your sick thoughts
To go and fulfill your own sick pleasures
You lost your soul taking away the gold
Along with all of their treasures
Your insecurities took advantage of the vulnerable
But you are a grown ass man
Who is supposed to be honorable
But you took the cookies and you ran
I am so mad at you for what you have done
Even though it has been decades ago
But God keep saying I have to forgive you
So that I can save my own soul
But I am still mad at you for what you have done
This is the purpose of this letter

To get it out and off of my chest
I thought It would have made me feel better
But at times I feel as if I have been robbed
When you faintly pop into my head
I be looking for an apology or accountability from you
But the life in you is gone, you're dead
So to make myself accountable for all of my mistakes
That I have done and will do as I live
And even though I am still mad at you
I want to say to you, I forgive.

LOH.LM.JH

PEOPLE THINK THEY KNOW ME

People think they know me,
But they really do not know who I am.
Just because we grew up as children,
Spending time together as friends.
Those times when I was down to do anything,
Just to make that score.
Sitting up in the trap house,
Sending dubs through a hole in the wall
Times when I thought it was all about me,
And I was fighting my battles alone.
Even though I was grown I still struggled,
Because I was unsown.
Yes, you must know the old me,
That held onto all of those grudges.
Yes, I held on to so much hate,
Always asking myself where the love is.
Yes, you knew the vulnerable me,
That would let you take advantage of
My trust, my faith, my loyalty,
My respect for you, and my love.
Just because you know the old me,
You think you know who I am
I ask to you who do you think I am,
Because I am not that person from back then
But when you now see me,
I am a judgement from your past

Reminiscing on all of the crazy things we did,
When we hung out together last
But then when you hear me talk,
And you are watching how I move
My presence to you seems different,
Yes I am somebody knew
So now when you see the new me,
You see someone who is more kind
Someone's whose weakness has turned into meekness,
And is loving all of the time
So now seeing the new me,
My presence to you may seem odd
Because I'm no longer a child of the streets,
I am a child of the most high God
The old me she was different,
Because she stayed in so much mess
But the new me she is redeemed, anointed
And she is definitely blessed
Now I am victorious,
I am fearfully and wonderfully made
I am now a seed of greatness,
Equipped with the tools God has gave I am also ready to become,
All God wants me to be
But if you do not know that,
Then you just do not know me

LOH.LM.JH